A CYCLE OF MYTHS

A Cycle Of Myths

NATIVE LEGENDS FROM SOUTHEAST ALASKA

COLLECTED AND EDITED BY

John E. Smelcer

A SALMON RUN BOOK

ANCHORAGE

MADE IN USA

Cover illustration by Larry Vienneau, Jr.
Design by Gregory E. Sowder, II
Artwork © 1993 Larry Vienneau, Jr.

Library of Congress Cataloging-in-Publication Data:

Smelcer, John E., 1963-
A Cycle Of Myths.
Bibliography: p.
Includes Index.
1. Alaska Native Mythology. 2. Oral Narratives.
3. Folklore. 4. Am. Indian—S. Alaska
I. Title

ISBN 0-9634000-2-9

A SALMON RUN™ *BOOK*
P.O. Box 231081
Anchorage, Alaska 99523-1081

Printed in the United States

Second Printing, 1995

"Wherever you go, I'll be with you;
Remember after all of the fire,
after all of the pain,
I will be the flame."

—Cheap Trick

In Memory of James Ernest Smelcer
(1965-1988)

Preface

This collection contains narrative myths and legends from the Eyak, Haida, Tlingit, and Tsimshian Peoples of Southeast Alaska. *The Raven And The Totem* © 1992 by the same author contains oral narratives from all of the remaining Alaska Native groups excluding Aleut. Together these books contain representative myths and legends from throughout Alaska.

Acknowledgements

This book is not only the product of my research and writing, much is owed to the many friends and colleagues who assisted me in some way, and I would like to thank those who helped.

Larry Vienneau, for his outstanding illustrations. I greatly admire his artistic abilities and count him and his wife, Suhtling, among my closest friends. Our various hunting and fishing adventures together are among my favorite recollections.

Tom Sexton, who reviewed the manuscript to this book. The turn-of-the-century photographs by the Mills Brothers are on loan to me from Tom, and I thank him for the use of them and for his continuing support.

Dr. Francis Sibley, my doctoral mentor and friend who also edited and reviewed some of the manuscript.

Dr. Michael Krauss, for special permission to use two Eyak narrative versions which I based primarily upon his earlier work with Anna Nelson Harry. I have the utmost respect for his linguistic research.

Dr. Alexandr Vaschenko, Director of the Gorky Institute of World Literature in Moscow, for reviewing the manuscript.

The University of Alaska Anchorage Consortium Library for special permission to borrow rare reference texts from its Alaska Collection.

Ahtna Heritage Foundation, for their scholarship support during my doctoral research, which in many ways was the basis for this book.

Andrew Stuart, my childhood friend, confidant, and brother whose spirit is in everything I do.

Robert Downes and his super-athlete daughter, Amy, whose humor and friendship is greatly appreciated.

Marie Smelcer, for her continued interest in my work and for reading the rough drafts to many of these narratives.

Charles Smelcer, for teaching me that honesty, integrity, and the respect for and of your family is the greatest achievement in life.

Herbert Smelcer, who more than anyone teaches me of my heritage and of the legacy of my family's history.

Lastly, I thank my wife and daughter. I become somewhat of a recluse while working on a project such as this, and because I was writing two books, I must have seemed like the Invisible Man. Pamela and Zara, your love means the world to me and I love you both with all of my heart.

CONTENTS

1

TLINGIT

2

HAIDA

3

EYAK

4

TSIMSHIAN

Introduction

The Alaska Native oral narrative traditions, that is, the orally trans-
mitted mythic and legendary folklore of the indigenous peoples, are as
rich and diverse as that of any literary tradition throughout the world.
Like the Babylonian epic the *Gilgamesh,* and the Homerian *Iliad* and
Odyssey, many of their stories come from deep antiquity where they
were first told orally hundreds, perhaps even thousands of years before
they were written. In this book are two such tales from the Tsimshian
which may be two thousand years old. Although not included in this
collection, there is an apparently far older story from Inupiaq Eskimo
about a shaman who encounters a ghostly band of hunters following a
mammoth across the frozen arctic tundra near the Kobuk River.

The oral narrative accounts from Alaska Native mythologies serve as
much more than simply good stories which hunters may have told to
one another while sitting about campfires watching the Northern
Lights in awe of its spectacular power and complex beauty. Anthro-
pologists, ethnographers, mythologists, and linguists have found that
they serve a significant function in preliterate societies. They describe
how the world was ordered, how things came to be, that is the origin-
myths of animals and places, how elements came to be, how to see and

1

identify objects, to explain the origin of things, to instruct, and to understand the history and value of native social and religious functions and events. As well, mythological narratives serve to teach language to native children, much as *Aesop's Fables* are read to children nowadays.

Perhaps most significantly, these traditional stories taught native people how to view and to relate to the world around them, especially in understanding the use of the natural resources which are so vital to their very survival. William Schneider, Director of the University of Alaska Oral History Program, wrote "For many of the Alaska Natives, oral narratives remain the primary source of all knowledge and of the transmission of cultural heritage." Mytho-narratives are significant in the psychological history and literature of all societies.

Myth is fundamental. It is the dramatic representation of our deepest instinctual life. It embodies in an articulated structure of symbol a vision of reality. It is the condensed history of a peoples' existence and attempts to represent reality with structural fidelity. Myths are, by nature, communal and collective, binding clans, tribes, and nations together. Myth is awareness of the universe. Myth dominates human experience. It is not an obscure or poetically complex means of expressing reality—it is the only means of expressing reality.

Although these mytho-narratives are hundreds and sometimes even thousands of years old, they are only more recently being recognized for the incomparable creations they are. Although Jesuit missionaries in the Seventeenth Century collected and translated a small number of Native American folktales, the current appreciation of Indian myth began in the United States with Henry H. Schoolcraft who, while visiting the Ojibwa Indians along the Mississippi River in 1822, commented on his elation at having discovered something altogether new and exciting in their traditional stories:

> Who would have imagined that these wandering foresters should have possessed such a resource? What have all the voyagers and remarkers from the days of Cabot and Raleigh been about, not to have discovered this curious trait, which lifts up indeed a curtain, as it were, upon the Indian mind, and exhibits it in an entirely new character?

And Elias Canetti, the Bulgarian Nobel Laureate of 1981, wrote:

> Tribes, sometimes consisting of just a few hundred people, have left us a wealth that we certainly do not merit, for it is our fault that they have died out or are dying before our eyes, eyes that scarcely look. They have preserved their mythical experiences until the very end, and the strange thing is that there is hardly anything that benefits us more, hardly anything that fills us with as much hope as these early incomparable creations. They have left us an inexhaustable spiritual legacy.

Tragically, the tradition which Schoolcraft and Canetti spoke so highly of is endangered. From the period of Russian contact until the mid-1900's, Alaska Native languages were severely depressed. Until 1972 native children were not permitted to speak their own language in school, and they were punished for doing so if caught. There are numerous accounts by native elders of how as children they were removed from their homes and placed in distant boarding schools where they were physically punished if found speaking the language of their family and ancestors. It was believed that by learning English and by abandoning their own language, that the native children would more easily become assimilated into Euro-American society.

It is estimated that the European "contact" with Native Americans is responsible for the devastation of as much as seventy percent (some estimations suggest eighty or ninety percent) of the pre-contact indigenous population, and that a similar demise has befallen their traditional languages.

In Alaska today, there are fewer than 120 native speakers in each of the following native groups: Han, Tsimshian, Haida, Ahtna, Deg Hit'an, Holikachuk, Upper Kuskokwim, Tanana, Tanacross, and Tanaina. Of great lament is the recent loss of the last fluent native Eyak speaker only this decade. Dr. Michael Krauss, a linguist at the University of Alaska Fairbanks' Alaska Native Language Center, and the last remaining fluent non-native speaker of Eyak, predicts that several native languages will be lost in the next two decades, and that most will be gone within fifty years.

According to Krauss, most responsible for the recent and the future deterioration of native languages transmission is the flood of radios and televisions now present in almost every rural Alaska home. It is this technological invasion, which he terms "cultural nerve gas," that most accounts for the demise of native languages and accordingly for native culture itself.

Ezra Pound, among the most influential poets of our century, once said that "Music rots when it gets too far from the dance. Poetry atrophies when it gets too far from music." There is real danger and concern that, like poetry, the magnificent narrative tradition of the first peoples of Alaska might also atrophy as the languages in which they were originally told become extinct. It is, after all, the language which gave birth to the narrative. The relationship between story and language is intricate and inseparable. The death of the one may quite possibly bear with it the death of the other.

O. W. "Jack" Frost, Professor Emeritus of Alaska Pacific University and my past mentor, wrote "Just as plant and animal species vanish from Earth far more rapidly than they are created, so the loss of language and culture is an extinction beyond full recovery." Clearly, whereas archaeologists can unearth artifacts to study and reconstruct past cultures, language only survives through successful transmission to living generations.

Although these mythological tales are undeniably significant, and certainly no one wishes them to become lost, there is an academic argument over just who should preserve them. On the one hand is the position that only native storytellers should tell, retell, or write the narratives. Accordingly, only natives of each culturally-unique group should tell the stories from their cultural heritage. In other words, an Ahtna Indian from the Copper River region should not write about or tell stories from neighboring Eyak (even if they heard the narratives from an Eyak), which seems to suggest that only Americans can write about American history, politics, or literature, and that only the English should write about Shakespeare and the Romantic poets.

Because the world is becoming a closer place, one in which we now recognize that we are more related to neighboring nations and peoples as a kind of global community, the exchange of cultural ideas, philosophies, and heritage is important. Although the Alaska Native myths belong ultimately to the native people, their survival may depend much upon their being disseminated to outside groups. Indeed, much of western society is built upon the exchange and enhancement of the literatures, arts, and technologies of other nations. The ultimate preservation of these myths and legends depends upon their being retold, and the world is a fitting audience to do just that. Just as the German folktales collected by Jacob and Wilhelm Grimm have survived by having been passed from one generation to the next, so too might these tales.

With this in mind, I set out several years ago to help in the preservation of the oral narrative "literature" tradition. Among the mythological tales found in this book, and those in my previous collection *The Raven And The Totem*, I have compiled eighty Alaska Native oral narratives with hope that by their being read, that they are somehow brought that much further away from the precipitous brink of what appears an ultimate extinction if the future is not altered from the course the past has set.

Although Tlingit linguist and former Alaska Poet Laureate Richard Dauenhauer has said that "it is no exaggeration to say that books are the tombstone of oral traditions," they may be, sadly, in the end, all that is left of the rich tradition which, as Elias Canetti wrote, has "left us an inexhaustable spiritual legacy." It is with such spirit, concern, and determination that I have compiled this book—that the beautiful and complex native languages and oral narratives of the Alaska Native Peoples will never perish from this earth.

A family of Alaska Indians at fishcamp somewhere along the Copper River. During the evenings the adults may well have told the stories which were handed down to them by their parents when they were young and at fishcamp. (Photo circa 1902 by Mills Brothers, courtesy of Tom Sexton)

Chief Stickwan (background) and a small band of relatives walking one of the extensive trails used by the Indians. Many of these routes had been used by the people for thousands of years. The seasonal travel patterns as natives moved between distant fishing and hunting camps and trading posts may account much for the broad dissemenation of oral narratives. (Photo circa 1902 by Mills Brothers, courtesy of Tom Sexton)

Alaska Native Languages And Peoples

Alaska Quarterly Review, Teacher's Guide.
Special Issue. Vol. 4, No. 3 & 4. Anchorage:
Alaska Humanities Forum, 1988.

TLINGIT-
HAIDA

Introduction To Tlingit And Haida

The Tlingit and Haida are maritime neighbors who occupy the mainland and islands of southeast Alaska. The traditional range of the Tlingit is one of the largest geographic areas of all Alaska Native Peoples. It extends to the west as far as 100 miles beyond Yakutat, while to the east it reaches as far as Ketchikan, only 50 miles from the British Columbia border. Some of the larger communities in the Tlingit region are Haines, Juneau (the state capital and Alaska's third largest city), Sitka, Kake, Wrangell and Ketchikan.

According to the demographic research of Dr. Michael Krauss, Director of the Alaska Native Language Center at the University of Alaska Fairbanks, who conducted a population census of Alaska Natives in 1974 and later revised it in 1982, and to more recent data, there are between 9-10,000 Tlingit in Alaska at this time. Of this number, fewer than 1,000 elders still speak the traditional language. Tlingit has the third highest population of natives after Central Yupik Eskimo (12,000) and Inupiaq (sometimes spelled "Inupiat") Eskimo (11,000).

The Alaska Haida have for many years lived in a rather small area on the southern most half of Prince of Wales Island, ten miles from the Alaska-British Columbia boundary. The largest Haida settlements are Hydaburg, Craig, and Klawock, although many Haidas live in Ketchikan. Their ancestral home is the Queen Charlotte Islands of British Columbia. According to their oral history the Haida, who originally lived on Langara Island off the northern tip of Graham Island in what is now British Columbia, moved to Prince of Wales Island two or three hundred years ago because food was so abundant there, and so they made the 25 mile journey in small boats.

11

According to Dr. Krauss and recent data, there are between 400-500 Haida in Alaska, and of these only some 40-50 elders still speak the traditional language. There are nearly twice as many Haida and Canadian Haida speakers in the Queen Charlotte Islands of British Columbia.

Tlingits and Haidas are known for their distinctive art, especially for their totem poles, an artform unique to Northwest Coast cultures. Of all Alaskan groups totem poles are found only among the Tlingit, Tsimshian, and Haida peoples. They are generally carved from cedar and are so ornately and intricately fashioned that the famous French anthropologist Claude Levi-Strauss once commented that as art they rival the art of ancient Greece. He was similarly impressed by the Tlingit-Haida formline artform.

(From: *The Native People of Alaska,* S. J. Langdon)

These magnificent totem poles were never worshipped as god-like dieties as some Judeo-Christian "Golden Bull," which many early missionaries to Alaska believed. Instead, they designated clan property and membership (Although the term "tribe" is sometimes used to describe the social organization of the Tlingits and Haidas, Dr. Steve Langdon, an anthropologist at the University of Alaska Anchorage, suggests that the term "clan" is the most accurate description). More generally, the animal characters and images depicted on the poles told entire mythic and legendary tales. Indeed, many of the Tlingit-Haida-Tsimshian narratives in this collection may be found portrayed in the totem poles of the region.

Both groups obtained much of their subsistence from the sea, and salmon, halibut, ling cod, and red snapper (an ugly but delicious rockfish) accounted for much of their diet. The mainland Tlingit sometimes hunted moose and mountain goat, while the island-bound Haida often hunted deer in the fall. In the winter months clams, mussels, and seaweed supplemented their diet.

Whereas Tlingit is somewhat related to other proto-Athabaskan languages, Haida, like Tsimshian, is an altogether different language and shares very little or no relationship to other Alaskan Native languages.

Russian explorers and traders first came into contact with these people sometime around the late 1700's, and the full invasion did not occur with great impact until 1800. It was not until the building of Sitka in 1805 that the Russians established a stronghold in the region. Before that, under the leadership of Chief Katlian, the Tlingits had run off the Russians in 1802 using firearms supplied to them by American and British traders in an attempt to rid the area of the Russians.

There are a great many oral narratives collected from these two groups because, like the Eskimo, there has been a popular fascination with Tlingit and Haida cultural artifacts (including their "stories") since the mid to late Nineteenth Century. The stories offered here are but a small representation of what has been recorded, and most of the Tlingit narratives in this volume have appeared in my previous book *The Raven And The Totem* (1992), although even those have under-gone some revision.

Raven, a central character in Northwest Native American Indian mythologies, is usually a selfish and greedy trickster, but he is also sometimes a creator, as is Coyote, the continental Native American Indian parallel to the Raven character.

Among the Tlingit narratives herein is the story depicting how Raven brought light into the world by stealing the sun, the moon, and the stars from a Tlingit chief on the Nass River. There is also a narrative of the genesis of the first killer whale, a powerful clan symbol in Tlingit-Haida society. In this collection are the Tlingit *Owl Legend* and *Fog Woman,* and the Haida narratives *Blackskin Meets Strength* and *Shag and Raven.* Like many native myths and legends, these tales are didactic, that is, they teach or instruct cultural moral lessons.

Most societies have some account of from where people first came. In certain legends from Africa, South America, and Australia mankind is brought up from the depths of the earth. In a Tlingit narrative man is made from clay. In this collection is the Haida tale *Raven and the First Haida People* which depicts how Raven first found humanity in a clamshell.

It should be noted that the oral narratives of the Tlingit and Haida, more so than with most other Alaska Native groups, are quite literally owned by specific clans as a kind of clan property. It is with great respect and admiration of their cultural tradition that I offer these narratives.

TLINGIT

Raven Steals the Stars, Moon, and Sun

Just as western religion suggests that the world was void of light in the beginning, so too was the Tlingit world before Raven stole the sun, the moon, and the stars and released them. There are ethnographic accounts of this narrative in Eskimo, Upper Tanana, Tanaina, Koyukuk, Deg Hit'an, Ahtna, Haida, and Tsimshian mythologies. In some versions Raven turns himself into a hemlock needle to impregnate the young woman, while in others he becomes a spruce needle, a small fish, and even a piece of fine moss. Recorded as early as 1850 in Sitka by Heinrich J. Holmberg, this version was told by Margaret McNeil, a Tlingit born in Juneau.

In the beginning there was no light. Raven, the most powerful of all beings, had made the animals, fish, trees, and humanity. He had made all living creatures. But they were all living in darkness because he had not made the sun.

One day Raven learned that there was a great chief living along the banks of the Nass River who possessed the sun, the moon, and the stars in a carved cedar box. The great chief also had a very beautiful daughter. Both the girl and the treasure were guarded well.

Raven knew that he must trick the villagers in order to steal their treasure, so he decided to turn himself into a grandchild of the great chief. He flew upon a tall tree near their house and turned himself into a hemlock needle. Then, disguised as the needle, he fell into the daughter's drinking cup. When she filled it with water, she drank the needle. Inside the chief's daughter, Raven became a baby and soon the young woman bore a son who was so dearly loved by the chief that he gave him whatever he asked for.

The stars, the moon, and the sun were each held in a beautiful and ornately carved cedar box which sat on the wooden floor of the house. The grandchild, who was actually Raven, wanted to play with the stars and the moon, and would not stop crying until the grandfather gave them to him. As soon as he had them, Raven threw them up through the smokehole. Instantly, they scattered across the sky. Although the grandfather was unhappy, he loved his grandson too much to punish him for what he had done.

Now that he had tossed the stars and the moon out the smokehole, the little grandson began crying for the box containing the sun. He cried and cried and would not stop. He was actually making himself sick because he was crying so much. Finally, the grandfather gave him the box. Raven played with it for a long time. Suddenly, though, he turned himself back into a bird and flew up through the smokehole with the box.

Once he was far away from the small village on the Nass River he heard people speaking in the darkness and approached them.

"Who are you and would you like to have light?" he asked them.

They said that he was a liar and that no one could give light.

To show them that he was telling the truth, Raven opened the ornately carved box and let sunlight into the world. The people were so frightened by it that they fled to every corner of the world. This is why there are Raven's people everywhere.

Now there are stars, the moon, and the sun and it is no longer dark all of the time.

The Creation Of The Killer Whale

The Killer Whale clan is one of the oldest of all Tlingit *clans.
This narrative tells how a mighty hunter named* Natsalane'
*created the killer whale for revenge. As with most myths and
legends, there are many variations of the story. This particular
version was told to me by* Heidi Rose, *a Tlingit from* Kake.

There once was a very mighty Tlingit hunter named Natsalane' who
could throw a spear and shoot an arrow better than any other. When
he hunted, he always killed the animal that he tracked. Whenever he
returned from a hunt the whole village would come out to see him because he always brought meat which he would share with everyone.

Now Natsalane' often hunted with his three brother-in-laws, and
together they often prepared for hunts. One day the brothers were
readying themselves for a seal hunt and they began to wonder.

"If it were not for Natsalane' we would be the best hunters in the
village and all the people would come out to see us when we returned
from a hunt," said the oldest of the brothers.

The second oldest brother agreed, and they planned to kill poor
Natsalane' while on the seal hunt.

The day the great hunt came, the hunters went to a small, rocky island which was exposed because the tide was low. But once the tide
came in the small island would be under water. There they left poor
Natsalane' to drown. As they paddled away, the youngest brother
begged the others not to kill their brother by leaving him there.

"Please, do not do this terrible thing," he pleaded as he tried to
turn around the canoe.

19

Natsalane' saw this, but the young brother failed, and so they left the great hunter to die alone on the island. Natsalane' watched as they faded into the distance, and he covered his face as the water rose.

Suddenly he heard a voice speaking to him. He opened his eyes but saw no one, only a loon floating nearby. Again he closed his eyes and again he heard the strange voice. This time he looked through his fingers and saw that it was the loon. Because loons are very hard to catch when they speak, Natsalane' was rewarded. The loon used his magic and made a hole in the water's surface. Under it was a place with many people who spoke his language. .t was the village of the Seal People.

The chief of the village led Natsalane' to the bedside of a sick and dying man. On the wall behind him was the picture of a powerful and terrible looking beast. Natsalane' asked the chief what it was and he replied, "It is the creature in your dreams."

Although the village shaman had tried to save the sick man he was sure to die very soon. The chief asked Natsalane' if he could help heal the man. The mighty hunter saw the shaft of a spear sticking from the man's side. Because it was made by a human, the Seal People could not even see it. Natsalane' carefully pulled it out of the dying man who was instantly healed.

Because he had saved the man, the chief agreed to help Natsalane' return home. He told him that he could get to shore if he only thought about reaching the beach and not about drowning or about the village under the sea.

The hunter thanked him and began to swim to shore. But halfway he turned and thought about what had happened at the small island and he started to drown. Quickly Natsalane' thought only about the beach and he soon made it there.

It took him several days to reach his village. He snuck into his house at night and told his wife to get his tools for him. He made her promise not to tell anyone that he was still alive—especially not his brother-in-laws.

That very night Natsalane' took the tools and walked far up the beach from the village and began his plan for revenge. He fell a great spruce tree and carved from it the horrible and powerful monster he

20

had seen in the Seal People's village, and he named it "Keet."

When he was finished, he sang and danced and spoke to it and pushed it into the sea. It was alive but it did not swim. In a few minutes it washed up on shore and died. It died because it did not have a spirit. But Natsalane' did not give up his plan. Instead, he fell a giant alder and carved from it the horrible whale-monster a second time. But it too did not live long. Natsalane' carved the beast a third time using red cedar. But it lived only slightly longer than the previous one.

Natsalane's anger at his brother-in-laws was tremendous. It burned hot in his heart. He sat for a long time thinking about the image he had seen in the sick man's house. It was almost midnight, the time when night turns over in its restless sleep, when Natsalane' carved the creature for the fourth time from a giant piece of yellow cedar drift-wood which was lying on the beach lit only by the moonlight which glowed off the smooth surface of the sea.

When he was done, he sang and danced and called it "Keet Shagoon," *Killer Whale*. He pushed it into the water, and it began to swim wildly showing its large, sharp teeth. Natsalane' bent close to his creation and spoke to it, "I made you to kill my brother-in-laws who tried to kill me. Kill the two, but spare the youngest one who tried to save me."

For six days Natsalane' and the killer whale waited and watched for the canoe of his brother-in-laws. Finally, the right canoe came by and the man told Keet to go do as he demanded.

Keet swam to the canoe as fast as an arrow, snapping his jaws and showing his terrible teeth. The men saw the great monster coming at them and they were terrified. Keet's powerful tail smashed the boat and the three brother-in-laws fell into the cold water. The killer whale attacked the two older brothers and ripped them into pieces. The sea turned red where the canoe had once been.

Natsalane' stood at the edge of the sea and watched the horrid scene. He saw how easily and perfectly his creation had destroyed the boat and killed the two men, and he was afraid.

When the evil brothers had been killed, Keet Shagoon brought the youngest brother safely to shore.

Now that he had his revenge, Natsalane' thought that he must do something about Keet who might kill many Tlingit halibut fishermen.

Natsalane' again spoke to the great killer whale, "I created you only to kill those who had done a great wrong to me. Now I will let you go. Because I am a man, you are never to kill another man again."

Keet looked at Natsalane' and he no longer looked so terrible. He turned and swam slowly away as his maker watched. The tamed monster became the totem symbol of the Killer Whale clan, and it has never killed a man since then.

L.VIENNEAU

The Owl Legend

Fish are an important resource of food to the Indians of Southeast Alaska, and the invention of the fish trap is certainly a significant development in native prehistory. This magical tale accounts for the creation of the first fish basket. As are many native legends, this narrative is didactic. That is, it teaches a moral lesson: Don't be selfish and don't mistreat your mother-in-law.

A young woman once lived with her husband and mother-in-law in a village where Sitka is today. The village was close to the sea and she often walked along the beach watching the waves as they crashed upon the rocks. During the herring and oolachan season, when the shallow waters were full of the shiny and oily fish, she watched how countless fish would be swept near shore by the tide but would then be washed away again as the tide receded.

She looked on and thought to herself, "There must be some way to catch these fish so that I will have plenty of food. What a waste that they are all washed away by the water."

She walked along the long beach still thinking about the problem. Just then she saw a dense patch of hemlock trees in the woods whose branches were so intertwined that they looked like a net.

This gave her an idea. She tore some branches from the hemlock tree and then ripped some long strips of bark from a nearby cedar. Using the wet bark strips like string, she fashioned the hemlock branches into a large basket-shaped net. With the basket in hand, she walked to where the fish were and waited for the tide to come in.

25

Finally, the high tide arrived and herring and oolachan were everywhere. She walked out into the sea up to her waist and dipped her basket beneath the waves.

"Come to your wife, fish," she said smiling.

When she brought it up, the basket was full of the shiny fish. She carried the heavy basket to the beach and poured the shimmering, wiggling herring and oolachan onto the sand.

Then, with her basket-net empty, she returned to the same place and caught even more fish. Every time she dipped the basket under the waves it came up full of fish. She was very happy because her idea worked so well.

Once she had caught enough fish, she hung most of them to dry and then she hid her invention in the woods where no one else would find it because she was greedy and did not want to share, especially not with her mother-in-law. She decided that she wasn't even going to give her any of the fish to eat.

That night the young woman waited until the mother-in-law was out of the house, and then she cooked some of the herring for herself and ate them all. But the mother-in-law smelled the fish and came into the house.

"What are you cooking, daughter-in-law?" she asked. "It smelled so good outside. What are you eating?"

The young woman swallowed her last bite and answered.

"Nothing," she said.

The very next day when her husband was seal hunting, she cooked another herring.

This time her mother-in-law came into the house before she had eaten all of the fish.

"I smell cooked fish again. You must be eating something. May I have a little to eat?" asked the old woman.

Although she had her basket-net and could catch many herring, the young woman was greedy and placed only fish entrails onto the cooking stick and cooked them for the mother-in-law and gave them to her.

"My son shall hear of how you have insulted and mistreated me and would have me go without food!" shrieked the old lady.

The young woman only ignored her. She was going to have all the fish she wanted and she wasn't going to share with anyone. After all, she thought, it was she who had invented the basket.

When her son returned from seal hunting, the mother-in-law took him aside and told him about his wife's cruelty.

The husband did not speak to his unkind wife, and so she went fishing again, but she could not find her basket. She had forgot where she hid it.

As darkness came she stood on the beach screaming, "Where is my basket? Give me my basket! Bring me my basket!"

She could see that the water was full of herring but she could not catch any of them.

She stood there still screaming and her voice was growing hoarse. "Where is my basket? Bring me my basket!"

No one answered her and she could not find the basket and the fish were laughing at her.

The young woman kept screaming until she could no longer make words. Her voice changed until she could only say, "Whoo... Who... Whoo..." Her arms changed into wings as she became an owl!

She flapped her wings and flew away hooting, "Whoo... Whoo... Whoo..."

Today, when a young girl is greedy her parents warn her that if she is selfish and mistreats her mother-in-law, that she will become an owl.

The Girl Who Was Taken By The Frog People

This particular telling of the Tlingit *legend of "The Frog Woman" is very similar to* J. R. Swanton's *account which he collected in 1904 outside* Wrangell.

There was a large village in the Yakutat country and not too far away there was a big lake full of frogs. In the middle of this lake there was a large swampy place where many frogs used to sit. One day the chief's daughter spoke badly to the frogs. She picked up a large one and made fun of it saying, "There are so many of you living here. I wonder if you do things like we do? I wonder if you get married and live together?"

When she went out of her house that night a young man came to her and asked, "Will you marry me?" The chief's daughter had rejected many men before, but she agreed to marry this one right away.

Pointing toward the lake in the distance, the man said, "That is where my father's house is and where we shall live together."

They walked to the lake and when they arrived, it seemed as though the edge of the water was lifted up like a blanket so that they could go under it. They walked beneath it. There were so many young people there that she did not think about going home again.

Meanwhile, her father and friends missed her and looked for her. But they did not think to look under the lake. Finally, they gave up and beat the drums and had a death feast. They painted their faces black and cut their hair as was their way.

In the spring, there was a village man who was going hunting. He went beside the lake to bathe himself in urine so that he

29

could hunt better. When he was done he threw the urine onto the beach and it landed among some frogs sitting there and they jumped into the lake. The next day he did the same thing but this time he saw the chief's lost daughter sitting in the swampy place in the middle of the lake. He dressed quickly and ran to the village to tell the chief what he had seen.

He told the girl's father and soon many villagers went to the lake to see if it was truly the missing young woman. When they saw that it was indeed her, the people brought gifts to trade for the girl's release. But the frog people would not give her up.

By and by, the chief thought of a plan and he called all of the men of the village together. He told them to dig trenches so that they could empty the water of the lake. The frog chief could see what they were doing and told his people.

The men worked and worked, dug and dug, until soon the lake water was almost gone. The frog chief asked the girl to tell the villagers to have pity on them and not to kill all of them. But they only wanted the girl and didn't harm the others.

Soon, the frogs were scattered all over and the people caught the girl and her frog husband. They released her frog husband and then took the girl back to the village.

When anyone spoke to the girl, she made only popping sounds like a frog. But after a while she was able to speak again and she told them how all of the frog people of the lake had floated away in the trenches and were lost. The chief's daughter would not eat at all, even though they tried everything. After a while they hung her upside down and the black mud which she had eaten while among the frogs came out of her. When the last of the mud came out, she died.

Because the girl was taken away by the frogs of that place, and because she died there, it is said that the frogs near Yakutat can understand Tlingit and some of the people can understand them.

Fog Woman

This Tlingit *story, also told by* Heidi Rose *of* Kake, *depicts the creation of salmon and fog. It also illustrates how men must treat wives with kindness and respect. I have found similar accounts of this legend in* Tanaina *and* Tsimshian.

One day Raven decided to get married, so he flew to the Tlingit chief, Fog-Over-The-Salmon, who had a beautiful, young daughter of marrying age.

The chief was happy that Raven wanted to marry his daughter but he warned him, "You must first promise to take good care of my daughter and to have respect for her. If you treat her badly she will leave you and never return."

Raven listened carefully to Fog-Over-The-Salmon and agreed to his demands and they were soon married. Raven flew to his village near the water with his bride on his back and they lived there all summer and fall. When winter came they were without food and they grew very hungry.

One rainy day after they had not eaten for some time, Raven's wife began to make a large basket.

"Why are you making a basket?" asked Raven. "We have nothing to put in it."

His wife did not answer him but kept on making the basket which was very large now.

That night they went to bed hungry again. But the next morning when Raven woke up he saw his wife sitting on the floor with both her hands in the basket, which was full of water. He looked to see what

31

she was doing and when she was done there were salmon in the basket. She had created the very first salmon!

Raven was very happy and so they cooked and ate the fish. Thereafter, every morning she did the same thing, and every morning the basket was full of salmon. Raven was never hungry and their house was full of drying salmon.

Soon, though, Raven began to quarrel with his young wife and forgot all of the wonderful things she did for him. Every day he fought with her more and more until he struck her with a large piece of dried salmon. He had forgotten the words of Chief Fog-Over-The-Salmon and was treating her very badly.

Because of Raven's mistreatment the beautiful young woman ran away along the beach. Raven gave chase and when he caught up he tried to hold her, but his hands went right through her as if she was mist. She ran away again and Raven followed. Every time he tried to grab her, though, his hands passed right through her and she could not be stopped.

She ran into the water and all of the salmon that she had made and dried followed her. As she walked further into the water her body began to turn into mist until she disappeared and became the fog.

Raven flew to his father-in-law, Chief Fog-Over-The-Salmon, and begged to have his wife returned to him.

The chief listened to Raven and then told him, "You promised to take care of my daughter and to give her respect. You did not keep your word and so she is lost to you. You cannot have her back."

When Raven Tricked Ganook

Although there are a great many oral narratives about Raven, there are very few about Ganook, *sometimes spelled* Khanukh, *who is said to be even older and more powerful. This particular retelling of the myth is based upon the version told to* Heinrich J. Holmberg *in* New Archangel *(Sitka) in 1850. It accounts for the creation of the rivers and lakes, and also tells how Raven became black.*

In the very beginning of time, Raven was not the only magical and powerful being. The most powerful of all was Ganook who was without beginning or end. Back then Raven was white. He was not black like he is now.

One day Raven met Ganook while canoeing upon the sea and they spoke together awhile.

"How long have you been living?" Ganook asked his brother.

"I have been alive since before the world stood in its place," boasted the white Raven.

Raven then asked how old Ganook was thinking surely that he was not as old as he.

"I have was born before the river came up from below," answered Ganook.

"Yes," said the astonished Raven. "You are older than I."

Suddenly, Ganook took off his hat and instantly a dense fog settled upon the surface of the sea which was so thick that Raven could not see before him. Raven became very scared and begged that Ganook make the fog disappear. He had done this to show Raven that he was more powerful.

33

Thereafter Ganook invited his white feathered brother to join him at his great house for a feast. There was a large stone box with a lid upon which Ganook slept at night. Inside was the only fresh water in the world. Ganook shared it with Raven and the greedy bird could not get enough of it because it tasted so good.

After the feast Raven began to tell stories of his wonderful adventures. He told many tales and soon Ganook fell asleep on the stone box lid.

The deceitful Raven thought quickly and decided to steal some of the water. He tricked Ganook by placing excrement underneath him and then awoke him saying how he had messed himself.

"Just look at yourself!" Raven exclaimed.

Ganook rushed out into the sea to bathe and while he was away Raven quickly removed the heavy lid and drank some of the sweet water. But before he could escape Ganook returned and saw what Raven was doing. He grabbed the bird and began to roast him over a fire. The smoke from the fire turned Raven all black.

Finally, Ganook released Raven who quickly escaped. As he flew, though, he dropped the water from his beak and where it fell upon the ground rivers, streams, and lakes formed.

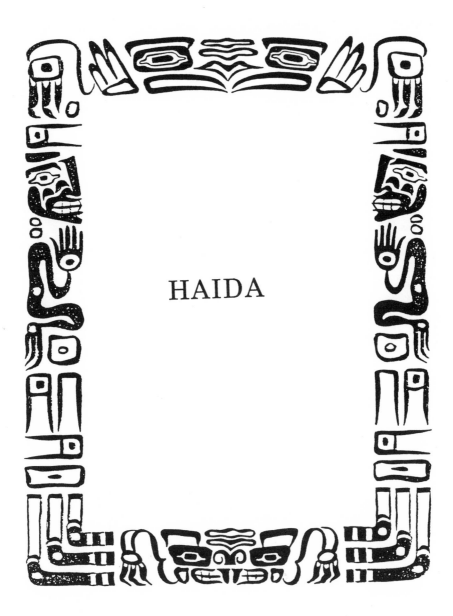

HAIDA

Raven and the First Haida

In this Haida narrative based upon a story told by Bill Reid *of* Hydaburg, *the genesis of the first Haida people is explained. In Tlingit mythology Raven also plays an important role in mankind's prehistory. In that story, however, he creates humanity from clay, while in this tale he merely finds them in a shell.*

A very long time ago there were no Haida in the world. There were no people anywhere. One day Raven was flying high over a beach when the tide was low. He landed so that he could eat whatever was exposed because he was always hungry. For a long time he just walked along the beach eating things until he became bored. The sun was shining on his black head and beak as he looked around for something to do.

All of a sudden he thought he heard a voice. He looked out over the water and saw nothing. He looked at the sky above him and then at the trees behind him, but he saw no one. He cocked his blue-black head and listened carefully.

When he heard the sound again it seemed to come from beneath him. Raven looked down at his feet and there was a large, white clamshell. The great magical bird picked it up and inside he saw many tiny creatures. They were all scared of him and so they huddled in the furthest corner of the gigantic shell.

Raven asked them to come out and play with him because he was so bored. The creatures were quite frightened, but eventually several of them came out of the clamshell and stood on the sand. They had never before been out of their house and the bright summer sun frightened them.

Raven looked closely at them. He had never seen such strange little creatures. They each had two skinny legs with no fur on them. Where Raven had great wings, they had two thin arms with neither fur nor feathers on them. These were certainly the most odd creatures Raven had ever seen. They were the very first people!

Raven played with them for a long time and he watched them and he taught them how to survive in the new world. Since that time, the Haida have lived along the beaches and have made their livelihood mostly from the sea, and they have never returned to live in the clamshell where Raven first found them.

Blackskin Meets Strength

One of the greatest of all Haida *and* Tlingit *mythological characters is the young* Blackskin, *their equivalent of the* Greek *mythological hero* Hercules, *and the* Judeo-Christian *hero* Samson. *There exist numerous accounts of his fantastic and heroic deeds.*

A long time ago, all of the men in a small coastal village wanted to be very strong so that they could hunt sea lions better. Each morning the men would run down to the sea and jump into the freezing water to bathe. This, it was thought, proved that they were strong.

Afterwards, they would all take turns trying to twist the giant tree in the center of the village. The strongest men would grab the trunk of the tree and twist with all of their might, but none could tear the tree from its deep roots.

The men of the village did many things so that they would become very strong.

The Chief of the village had a young nephew named Blackskin who would one day become chief. But the young man did not behave as a young chief-to-be should. He did not try to show off his strength by twisting the giant tree. He always slept during the day and he did not bathe in the very cold sea water with the other young men of the village. He earned his name because he always slept too close to the fire.

All of the villagers laughed at Blackskin because he was so weak and lazy. His own family, especially his two brothers, was ashamed of him. His brothers always called him weakling and lazy.

39

But Blackskin was neither of these things. Instead, he went and bathed alone in the water at night when everyone else was asleep, and he was becoming very strong. His uncle once noticed him leave the village at night and not come home until the next morning before everyone was awake. He knew that Blackskin was strong and could endure the icy cold water longer than any other man in the village.

Although the rest of the village still thought him to be a weak coward, Blackskin was a good man. He did not steal or lie, and he always gathered wood for the elders to keep their fires burning.

Each night when everyone was asleep he returned to the sea and he bathed there alone in the ice cold water lit only by the pale moonlight. He grew stronger and stronger, but he did not want to tell anyone how strong he was becoming.

One day a terrible hunting accident happened. A group of men had gone sea lion hunting, and when they were fighting one large bull, its powerful tail hit the Chief and killed him. His body was brought back to the village where a funeral ceremony befitting a chief was given in his remembrance.

Many stories were told during the ceremony of great legendary heroes who held great honor in their village. Blackskin enjoyed these stories and never tired of hearing them. He hoped that he too would one day bring great honor to his people.

Once the eight day funeral ritual was over, the men of the village vowed to return and kill the sea lion who had killed the chief. But first they had to prepare for the hunt and train their bodies by enduring the cold water. They also hit one another with branches to learn to endure pain and to toughen their skin

Fearing that others would laugh at him as they always had, Blackskin did not join them. Instead, he decided to avenge his uncle's death alone because he was certain that the uncle had been proud of him. So, every night he would endure the cold sea water alone.

His aunt noticed his secret and encouraged him to stay in the water longer and longer each night so that he would gradually build up his stength. Sometimes he would stay in the water so long that he could barely even crawl onto the shore. He switched himself with a branch harder and harder until his skin blistered, but he endured the pain. He was becoming very strong indeed!

One night when Blackskin was bathing alone he saw a man wearing a bearskin walking on the beach. He had never before seen the man and so he asked who he was.

"I am called Strength," said the man. "I have come to help you."

The stranger told Blackskin to fight him to test how strong he was. But when the chief-to-be approached him, the little man grabbed him, picked him up over his head, and then threw him hard onto the sand. Blackskin was astonished.

He wrestled with the bearskin-clad man several times, but each time he was defeated by the bandy-legged stranger.

"You are not strong enough yet," said Strength. "You must train more and then you will be ready to pit your strength against the village tree. I will help you, but you must not tell anyone that you have seen me."

Back in the village, the other men would wrestle to train themselves, but whenever Blackskin wrestled he always let himself be beaten because he didn't want anyone to know of his great strength. Most of the time he would just sleep during the day because he was so tired from training alone all night.

Everyone kept making fun of him, calling him lazy and weak. One night, when Blackskin was bathing in the cold sea, the small man called Strength returned and invited him to wrestle again. This time Blackskin threw him to the ground!

"You are strong!" exclaimed Strength. "Now you are ready to twist the giant tree."

So the small man led Blackskin through the dark to where the village tree grew. Blackskin hugged the tree's trunk with both arms and twisted it right out of the ground!

"Now," said Strength, "replace it in the ground as it was. You are ready to fight and kill the sea lion who killed your chief. You are stronger than the North Wind."

The next morning, the men of the village bathed as usual and then went to try the tree. Blackskin's oldest brother was first to try the tree. He twisted it out on the very first try.

All of the men shouted, "We are ready! Our training is complete!

Now we can go hunt the sea lion!"

Blackskin smiled when he heard this. But he did not tell anyone that he had twisted the tree in the night.

The next day the men were preparing their longboat for the trip and only the strongest men who had been training were chosen to go on the hunt.

Although he was not chosen, Blackskin was determined to be the one to avenge his uncle's death and kill the sea lion. He went to the wife of his uncle and asked her for the ancestral weasel-spirit hat which brought honor to the clan. She gladly gave it to him and was proud that he had asked for it. The other men, especially the two brothers, had not thought to wear the hat of honor.

Blackskin cleaned himself and dressed in fresh clothes and then walked down the beach to where the men were preparing to leave for the hunt.

When the others saw him, they were surprised. No longer was Blackskin the dirty, sooty young man they had always teased. Instead, he stood before them tall and confident wearing clean clothes and the ancestral hat. But nonetheless, they did not agree to let him join them.

Laughing, they pushed the long boat from the shore and began to paddle away. But Blackskin held the boat and kept it from moving although all the men paddled as hard as they could. Then Blackskin lifted the entire canoe with all of the men in it right out of the water and onto the beach!

The men thought that the tide must have washed the boat ashore. Surely, they thought, Blackskin had not done this.

The young chief-to-be asked if he could at least be the one to bail the water out of the craft. Because Blackskin was, after all, the nephew of the dead chief, the men agreed that he could go along.

They looked at Blackskin as he stepped into the canoe and one asked him, "How many sea lions are you going to kill?"

Blackskin didn't say a word. He climbed in and sat down in the bottom of the boat and went to sleep.

Finally, the hunters reached the island where the sea lions lived. As the boat approached the rocky shore, the oldest brother jumped out. Sea lions were all around him. He killed several smaller animals as he made his way to the big bull. When he reached the bull, the oldest brother tried to twist its head off as he had twisted the tree in the village, but the giant sea lion threw him down and smashed him against the rocks, killing him as it had killed the chief.

Then the other brother tried to kill the sea lion bull, but it killed him as well.

The other men became afraid and wanted to leave.

"If the big bull had so easily killed the two brothers," they thought, "then surely it can kill us as well."

They pushed their canoe off the island and started to leave. But Blackskin stood up in the canoe and spoke bravely as a chief speaks.

"Turn the canoe around and take it back to the island. I will kill the great bull and avenge my brothers and uncle."

They had never before seen or heard him speak or act like this and they saw that he was sure and confident. They realized that a chief had spoken and so they turned around and returned to the island.

Blackskin stepped out of the boat and went after the great bull who had killed his uncle and brothers. He grabbed many smaller ones by their tails and picked them up and dashed their heads against the rocks. When he finally came upon the giant bull, he wrestled with it and picked it up over his head and threw it to the ground as he had done to Strength. Then he twisted its head off and tore the dead sea lion in half with his bare hands!

The other men were impressed and amazed. They had never before seen such strength in a man.

When he had killed the bull, Blackskin collected all of the sea lions that he had killed and filled the boat with their bodies. There was plenty of meat for everyone in the village. The men were amazed and scared and returned home vowing to never again say mean things about Blackskin.

The news of his strength and courage, and of the honor he had be-stowed upon the village soon spread and Blackskin was made chief. Throughout his life, he accomplished many great things and always brought honor to his people, and he only used his great strength for good. He was truly a great man.

Shag and Raven

"Shag" is more commonly known as the cormorant, a large seabird. A Tlingit version of this story appears in The Raven And The Totem. *A similar account of this Haida narrative was collected by* Vesta Johnson *and told by* Victor Haldane, a Haida *from* Hydaburg, Alaska. *The moral of this story is quite clear: "Don't believe everything you hear."*

It happened one day that Raven, the Trickster, was flying along the coast when he came upon a small village. He was very hungry so the big, black bird landed.

Nearby, Raven saw Shag, the sea cormorant, and asked him to go halibut fishing. They took one of the Haida's boats and paddled out into the sea. While they paddled the canoe, Raven kept saying how great a fisherman he was and how would certainly catch more fish than Shag.

Once they started fishing in deep waters, though, the cormorant kept catching halibut. For a long time Raven did not bring in a single fish! He was angry because he had bragged that he was the better fisherman and here he had not caught a halibut while Shag had filled the canoe with his catch.

It began to get late, so the two birds started their return to the small village. Raven knew that he would be disgraced if the people learned that he had not taken any halibut. He thought of a trick to keep them from learning and then a plan came to him.

"What is that on your tongue?" he asked Shag.

The cormorant did not know what the black bird was talking about.

"Let me see your tongue," demanded Raven.

Shag stuck out his tongue and instantly Raven grabbed it and cut it out!

Then Raven said, "Let me hear you speak."

But Shag could not, even though he tried very hard.

When they arrived at the village with their halibut, the people were amazed. They had never before seen so many fish. As Raven threw each large halibut out of the canoe he told the villagers how he had caught it and how much of a fight it had put up. The sea cormorant was very angry and tried to speak, but because he could not he just jumped about.

Raven kept pulling halibut from the canoe saying how he had caught them all and how Shag was lazy and had not taken a single fish. This made the cormorant even more angry, but all he could do was jump about flapping his arms all over the place.

The Haida asked what was wrong with Shag.

"He is trying to tell you that I almost lost my life fighting that big one there," replied Raven pointing to a rather large halibut.

All of the villagers thought that Raven must certainly be the greatest fisherman. Shag became so mad that he attacked Raven, but the sly bird escaped and flew away. To this day the cormorant sits on rocks near the sea and he cannot speak because Raven cut out his tongue long ago.

The Devilfish

The Devilfish *is more commonly known as the octopus. With its many tenacles, it is easy to understand how the beast may have been given such a name. Narratives about octopuses are prevalent among southeast Alaska native mythologies. There are stories in Eyak, including* The Octopus Who Married a Woman *told by* Galushia Nelson, *and* The Giant Devilfish *told by* Old Man Dude. *This Haida version was told by* George Hamilton, Sr. *of* Craig *who died in 1984 at the age of 101, and it is said to have occured in* Devilfish Bay *at* Cape Chacon *on southeast* Prince of Wales Island.

About two or three hundred years ago there was a small Haida village at Devilfish Bay. It didn't have that name back then. One day a man and his son went seal hunting. They would kill many hair seals because they needed the meat to eat, the fur for clothing, and the oil for their lamps and for cooking. They hunted for several days.

While they were out hunting, a giant sea monster, a devilfish, came out of the water and destroyed the small village and dragged some of the Haida into the sea with it as it left.

When the man and boy returned they found their entire village had been swept out into the bay. There was slime all over the place. The man realized that a giant devilfish had done this. The two jumped into their boat and followed the trail of bodies that the octopus had dropped on its way to its underwater lair. The trail brought the two to the face of a great cliff. Just barely under the water they could see the terrible monster sleeping in its den.

They decided to return to camp to cut up their seal meat as bait for

47

the devilfish. When they had done this, they paddled back to the cliff and climbed up the side a ways. This done, they threw the seal into the water and waited. Soon, the giant octopus came up to eat the meat. The man took his long knife and jumped right off that cliff and onto the devilfish's back!

He stabbed and stabbed with his sharp blade. The monster's long tenacles went every direction trying frantically to dislodge the man. Slime covered everything and the water was thick with black ink.

In an instant the creature dived beneath the water with the hunter still on his back. When the surface stopped boiling and churning, the boy saw that his father was gone! He climbed down to the edge of the cliff and yelled for his father. As it grew late, he built a fire and sat there alone looking out over the sea.

After a while the giant devilfish floated up to the surface and was carried to shore by the waves. The boy took his knife and cut open the beast to take out its heart. As he did, his father stepped out of the octopus and embraced his son. He had killed the devilfish and since that time the place has been called Devilfish Bay.

Eagle-Man's Revenge

Although this particular narrative was retold by John Enrico, a Canadian Haida from Masset, versions of the story are found in the mythology of Alaskan Haida as well. With only 25 miles separating the two native groups it is understandable that they could share a common oral narrative. Revenge tales, like this one, are common in almost all cultures. A representative story from the Western literary tradition would be Hamlet.

Once, a long time ago, there was a young man who was trained by his uncle, as was then the custom. The young man did not listen well when he was being instructed and this frustrated the uncle. When it was clear that he would never learn anything, the uncle made a plan to kill him. He and several villagers made a large box with a great and heavy lid. One night they threw the young man inside it and closed the lid. They put the box in a canoe and sent it off into the sea.

Although he tried desparately to escape, the young man could not. The canoe drifted for many days, and the prisoner became very weak because there was no food or water inside the box.

Finally, the canoe came to rest on a small island. Two girls who were walking along the beach saw it. As they approached they saw the large box, too. They tried to lift it from the canoe but it was too heavy for them. They used their knives to pry off the lid and inside they saw the handsome young man who was nearly dead from lack of food and water. The took him to their father who was Chief of the Eagle People.

At his house the two beautiful girls helped the young man regain his strength. When he was strong enough, the chief told him that he must marry one of his daughters. The young man did this and for a long time he was very happy.

After a while he began to think about his wicked uncle who had tried to kill him. He told his father-in-law what his uncle had done to him and the chief agreed to help. He went to a large, carved cedar box and inside were many eagle skins with all of their feathers attached. The chief gave the young man one and told him to place it over himself. When he had finished dressing, the chief told him that he was now an eagle and that he could fly.

The young eagle-man thanked his father-in-law and flew off for the village where his uncle lived. When he arrived he landed upon a tree near the village and waited for his uncle. Several young boys saw the eagle and tried to cut down the tree to take his feathers. But every time the tree was about to fall the young eagle-man safely flew to another tree.

Finally, the wicked uncle came nearby. The eagle-man swooped down and grabbed him by his hair and flew away. The uncle struggled and yelled, but he could not free himself from the strong talons. He began to beg for his release. The young eagle-man told him who he was and he also told him what had happened after the box landed on the small island.

Although the uncle begged forgiveness, the eagle-man continued to fly far out over the ocean and there he dropped him into the water because of his cruelty.

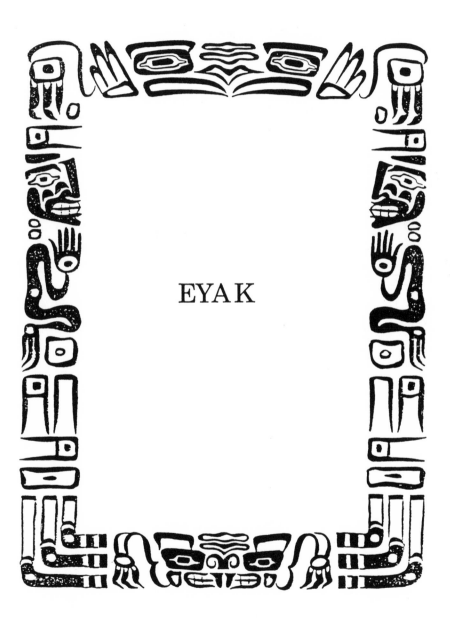

EYAK

Introduction To Eyak

The Eyak (pronounced ē ak) people have traditionally lived along a very short stretch of southeast Alaska coastline, ranging generally from Cordova to Yakutat, and along the lower Copper River Delta (a range of less than 100 miles).

The Aleut live to the west of Eyak territory, while to the east live the Tlingit. Both groups have played dramatic roles in the history and prehistory of the Eyak people. Whereas relations with Aleut were generally unfriendly, just the opposite was true with their neighbor to the east.

Unlike their coastal neighbor, the Tlingit, the Eyak were not a sea-going society. Instead of sea mammal hunting and halibut fishing, Eyak were gatherers, collecting clams and mussels at low tide. They fished the freshwater streams for salmon, and occasionally hunted mountain goats.

The linguistic structure of Eyak and Tlingit are somewhat related and this permitted co-existence between the groups. Indeed, the Tlingit, being a larger and more powerful group, easily assimilated the Eyak until the Tlingit language replaced that of the Eyak. However, although there are similarities in the linguistic structure of the two languages, the actual origin of Eyak is still questioned. Eyak is considerably more related to the Athabaskan languages of the interior, including those of northwestern Canada. Indeed, both Navajo and Apache is somewhat related to Eyak. All this suggests that at one time the Eyak may have been part of the proto-Athabaskan language family as are those of Arizona and New Mexico. However, the origin of their language aside, just when and where the Eyak people moved from to the coast remains a mystery.

Although contact has existed between Eyak and Europeans (Russian Americans mostly) since the late 1700s and early 1800s, there was relatively little contact until 1889 when four American canneries were established at Cordova in Eyak territory. This marked the beginning of the ultimate destruction of the native people.

Although Lt. Henry T. Allen (USA) encountered Eyak along the Copper River while on his reconnaissance mission (in which his findings were later published in *Report of an Expedition to the Copper, Tanana, Koyukon Rivers, in the Territory of Alaska, in the Year 1885*), the first anthropological-linguistic work performed in Eyak territory was in 1933 when Danish anthropologist Kaj Birket-Smith and Frederica de Laguna spent 17 days in Cordova between late April and early May. The oral narratives they collected at the time was published by the Danish Royal Scientific Society in 1938. The collection, entitled *The Eyak Indians of the Copper River Delta, Alaska* serves even now as a primary source of knowledge of the Eyak people, including their oral narrative myths and legends.

Kaj Birkit-Smith and Frederica de Laguna (right) in Cordova, 1933

54

In 1974 Michael Krauss, a linguist from the University of Alaska Fairbanks who first studied the Eyak in 1961, and author of *In Honor Of Eyak* (1982), compiled a demographic study of Alaska Native Peoples and their languages. He revised his data in 1982 after another census, and he found that only 2 native speakers of Eyak still survived. By the end of the year following the project, Anna Nelson Harry died and in February of 1992 Sophie Borodkin died, leaving no native speaker of Eyak in existence! Dr. Krauss has been working with Marie Smith in hopes of rekindling the language.

Because of the unfortunate demise of the language, and because so very little was documented prior to that demise, any newly discovered translations, manuscripts, or audio recordings is *extremely* significant. Whereas hundreds of Eskimo (both Alaskan and Canadian) myths have been documented, primarily due to contemporary public interest, only a handful of narratives in Eyak have ever been recorded.

The oral narratives contained herein, particularly *The Blind Man and the Loon,* and *The Octopus Who Married a Woman,* have both been told before (in 1933 to the Birket-Smith-de Laguna expedition and later in 1965 to M. Krauss). It is with thanks to Michael Krauss for special permission to reprint these versions which are so much based upon his translations.

The narrative *When Raven Killed The Whale,* is based, in part, upon the account told by Galushia Nelson around 1938, and upon my own research of neighboring Indian mythologies. *Raven and Loon: The Necklace Story* was told to me by my own beloved grandmothers, Mary Wood-Smelcer and her sister Morrie Second-chief. My wife and I were caribou hunting in the Ahtna Mendeltna area and we visited Morrie in her home there. The two women jointly told us this narrative. I wish I had had my video camera with me—such was the magic of that particular telling. I include it in this chapter not only because Ahtna is such a close geographic neighbor to Eyak (although their languages have no commonality), but because similar versions of the narrative exist in Eyak mythology as well.

The Blind Man and the Loon

The story of The Blind Man and the Loon *is perhaps one of the most common of Alaska native myths, second only to* Raven Steals the Sun, Stars, and the Moon. *Accounts of this story appear in* Yupik, Inupiaq, Upper Tanana, Tanaina, *and* Ahtna *ethnography. Like many narratives, it teaches a moral lesson: "Don't be greedy and be kind to those less fortunate."*

A husband and wife once lived inland along the Copper River. The husband was blind and so the wife had to work hard to gather enough food for them. Because the man was blind, the two had not had any game meat for a long time. One day, though, the wife saw a large moose walking by.

"A moose is walking by," she whispered.

"Quick," said the husband, "hand me my bow and arrows."

The wife gave them to him. Because she was not strong enough to draw back the bowstring, she had to let the husband shoot. But because he could not see, the wife had to guide his aim.

"Is that good?" he asked her. "Am I aiming at the moose?"

"Yes," she replied. "You are aiming correctly."

The blind man let loose the arrow and instantly he heard the unmistakable sound of the arrow striking the animal's side. The heavy moose lurched forward but then fell down dead.

The wife did not tell him the truth. Instead, she had a plan.

"Quick, husband," she said, "it is running away. Shoot again."

The wife helped him aim again. But this time the arrow hit the ground because there was no moose where she had pointed him. She lied to him saying how poorly he had shot.

"You missed it! It got away! she said insultingly.

She told him to stand where he was while she gathered the two arrows. The wife pulled the bloody arrow from the moose's side and wiped it clean in the grass. Then she stuck it in the mud along the riverbank and took it back to her blind husband.

He smelled the tip. "It smells like blood," he told her.

"No," she replied. "You only hit the mud. You did not kill the moose."

She took her husband back to their camp near a small lake behind the river. Then she went back to cut off pieces of the moose for herself. She was not going to tell him the truth. She was going to eat all of the meat and not share any with him.

Soon after, the blind man heard a voice coming from the lake.

"Come here," it said.

This startled the man because he did not know anyone was there.

He stood and answered the voice, "I am blind, I cannot see."

The strange voice spoke again, " Come here. You can feel your way."

The man cautiously found his way to the lake's edge. It was a giant loon which was speaking to him. It spoke to him again.

"Sit down on my back and hold on to my neck feathers."

The blind man did as he said and the loon dove under the water with him and swam around the lake twice. When he came up for air, the loon spoke to him.

"Now, look around," it said.

The man opened his eyes.

"I can see a little," he said excitedly.

"Close your eyes again and hold your breath," demanded the loon.

This done, the two dove under water again and swam around the lake once more. This time when the loon came up the blind man could see perfectly! He thanked the magical bird and walked back to find his wife to tell her the good news. When he found her he saw that she was boiling some meat and he saw the dead moose that he had killed in the bushes beside her. She had lied to him and now she was not even going to share the food with him. This made him very angry.

When the wife saw him she nervously said, "I was just cooking

58

some meat for you."

The husband was so mad because she had tricked him that he shoved her head into the boiling pot and killed her.

From then on he always had good luck and was a great hunter.

The Octopus Who Married A Woman

As stated in the Introduction *to this chapter, very few Eyak oral narratives have ever been recorded. This particular re-telling of the story of* The Woman and the Octopus *has appeared in Michael Krauss'* In Honor Of Eyak, *in* Northern Tales, *by Howard Norman, and in John F. C. Johnson's* Eyak Legends.

One day a young Eyak woman was wading along the beach with her child on her back. She was looking for shellfish and other things to eat which might be left on the beach while the tide was out.

She walked out to where the water was up to her waist when something started pulling on her leg. Something under the water was grabbing her!

She started to call for help, but no one was near and no one saw what was happening. Her child began crying. As she was pulled into deeper water, the young woman pushed her child away from her and told him to swim for shore.

"Tell your uncles what has become of me!" she yelled as the child swam to safety.

That was her last breath of air because the water was now over her head and she was certain that she would drown. When the woman looked, she saw that it was a large octopus which had her leg and now was pulling her towards a cave.

When they went inside she saw that it was actually a house and the octopus had turned into a man. He told her that she was to be his new wife.

For a long time they were married and they were happy. Everyday

the man would go out and catch fish to bring back to his family. The woman had two children by him. They were really octopus-children, but she loved them very much.

One day while her husband was fishing, the woman swam up the surface and was sitting on a rock, watching the waves crash upon the shore, when her brothers walked by and saw her sitting there.

They could not believe their eyes. There was their long lost sister. They came out to where she was and told her that they would take her home.

"Come," they said, "it is time for you to come home with us.

The woman replied, "I cannot. My husband would be angry if you took me away and he would hunt you on the sea and kill you."

Before they left, the woman invited them to come and visit sometimes.

When her octopus-husband came home she told him that her brothers wanted to take her home.

"I told them that I would not go yet because you would be angry," she said while he cooked the food in his usual way.

The husband was pleased that she had stayed.

"You must tell them not to kill me or my brothers. Those men are always killing. That is what they always do," he said to his wife.

One day they both decided to go visit her relatives on land. The people were happy to see her and her two sons. They did not know that the husband was an octopus and that the children were really octopus-children.

They lived in the village for a long time and one day while hunting whales with his new brother-in-laws, a large whale killed the octopus-man.

The wife was very sad. She was so heart-broken that she died soon afterwards from the grief.

The two sons jumped into the water and turned into giant octopuses and they swam out to sea and killed that whale to avenge the death of their parents. After that, they never returned to the small village.

When Raven Killed The Whale

I have collected versions of this narrative in Tlingit, Tanaina, Upper Tanana, and Koyukon Athabaskan. *That similar accounts exist in Interior Alaska Indian mythologies suggests that exchange of goods and information, to include stories, was predominate among the various indigenous populations. This* Eyak *story, which is based upon a tale told by* Galushia Nelson, *differs only slightly from the Athabaskan narratives.*

One day Raven was flying high over the ocean looking for something to eat. As usual, he was very hungry. He was flying around when he saw a killer whale swimming below.

Raven flew down close and thought of a way to trick and eat the whale. He saw how that every time the whale came up to breathe, its blow-hole would open. He decided to fly into the hole the very next time he could. But when he tried, the conniving black bird found that he was too big to go down the hole.

Finally, an idea came to him. Quickly Raven flew away to shore and collected some firewood which he bundled together in birch bark. Then he went back to the whale and spoke to it.

"Cousin Whale," he said. "I have come to tell you that we are relatives."

"That is impossible," replied Whale. "I am a killer whale and you are a bird. We cannot be cousins."

Raven thought about a suitable answer and then responded, "But I can prove to you that we are indeed cousins."

"How can you prove it?" asked the curious whale.

Again, Raven thought very quickly. He was a very good trickster.

"Open your mouth," he said, "and I will show you how our throats are exactly the same shape."

Although he did not trust him entirely, Whale nonetheless opened his great mouth. Once it was opened far enough, Raven ran into his mouth and down his throat.

Once inside, Raven cut some meat from the whale with his knife and built a fire to cook it using the firewood he had collected. As soon as Raven began to cook the meat, Whale smelled the fire and knew that he had been tricked. He begged the great bird not to eat his heart and liver. Raven agreed, and so for many days he lived there inside the whale eating his meat whenever he was hungry, which was most of the time.

One day when the whale was close to shore, Raven cut out the liver and heart and ate them. Whale died instantly and was washed ashore by the waves. Raven stayed inside the killer whale for two more days eating a hole through the rib cage. On the third day he walked out of the whale and flew away to find something else to eat.

Raven and Loon: The Necklace Story

I have collected many Alaska Native oral narratives in the past several years, but this particular Ahtna Athabaskan version of a popular native myth, is one of my favorites as it was told to me in Mendeltna by Mary Wood-Smelcer, my grandmother, and her sister, Morrie Secondchief. There was a magical quality to the telling as both women recalled the story from their youth and took turns telling segments and seeking affirmation from the other. Versions of this narrative can be found in the mythologies of many North American Indian groups, including Eyak, which is a neighbor of Ahtna.

In the time very long ago, when animals could speak and people had not yet been created, Raven and Loon were good friends and visited with one another often. Back in those days both birds were white. They were white all over.

One day Raven was flying and he saw Loon swimming on a lake. He landed and asked his friend to come and visit him. The other bird swam to shore to talk with his friend.

"Let's paint each other," said the white Raven.

They looked around and found some black mud and with it Raven began to paint the white Loon's back and feathers black with white speckles, and then he made a pretty necklace around Loon's neck.

"Oh, you look so wonderful!" Exclaimed Raven when he was finished.

Loon looked at himself in the lake's reflection and saw how pretty he was, and that he had a beautiful necklace. But his head and chest was still white.

Raven asked his friend, "Please, paint me just as I have painted you so that I will look as pretty."

Loon took some mud and began painting, but he was not as good as Raven and he could not make him as pretty. He tried very hard, but he could not paint as well.

When he was done Raven looked at himself in the water and saw that he was all black, even his feet, head, and beak was black. He did not even have a necklace around his neck. He began to jump up and down and to yell at Loon.

"Look at me! Look at me!" he screamed. "I am all black. You did not paint me like I painted you. I do not even have a pretty necklace!"

The angry Raven chased Loon all over trying to get him. All that time the loon was saying that he was sorry.

Finally, Loon flew out to the middle of the lake where his angry friend could not get him. Raven stood on the beach and shouted, and then he picked up a handful of mud and threw it and hit Loon right on the head. When he was tired of yelling, Raven flew away and they have not been friends again.

Since that time, Raven has been black all over and Loon has a black head and a pretty necklace.

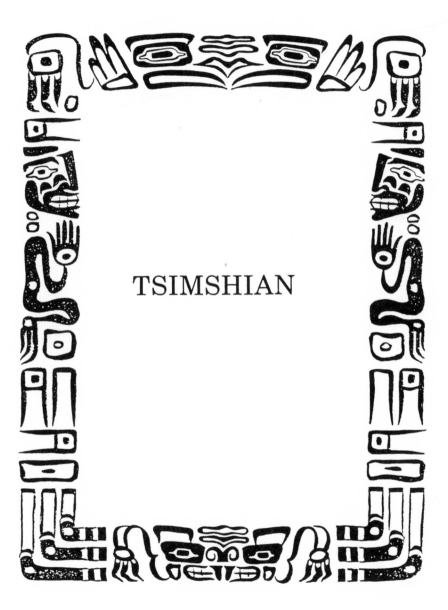

TSIMSHIAN

Introduction To Tsimshian

The Tsimshian people of Alaska have traditionally lived in an area ranging from the now-existing island village of Metlakatla, inland to Kinkolith along the Nass River and continuing southeast along the Skeena River in British Columbia. Their neighbors to the northwest were the Alaska Tlingit and Haida Indians, while to the southeast were the Kwakiutl, Bella Bella, and Bella Coola Indians of British Columbia and northern Washington.

In Alaska, however, their only surviving stronghold is the small community of Metlakatla on Annette Island which measures less than 250 square miles, across from Prince of Wales Island (which is traditional Tlingit-Haida territory). Although some Alaska Native groups have smaller populations (e.g. Han, Ahtna, Tanana, Tanacross, Upper Kuskokwim, and Holikachuk), Tsimshian is confined in the smallest geographic region.

Of the twenty culturally unique Alaska Native groups, the population of more than half are better represented than is Tsimshian. According to the demographic research of Dr. Michael Krauss (Director of the Alaska Native Language Center, University of Alaska Fairbanks), less than 1,000 Tsimshian exist in Alaska (almost entirely represented in Metlakatla), and of those less than 100 elders over age 50 currently speak the language (it is significant to note that in most native groups it is the elders alone who still speak the languages. Krauss blames this on the influence of television). It is possible to predict (based especially upon the recent history of the Eyak) that very few, or indeed no native speaker of the language will survive the next 20-30 years.

In Canada, however, the number of Tsimshian people and native speakers is much greater. According to Krauss' census, there were over 9,000 Canadian Tsimshian, and some 3,500 spoke the language. Undoubtedly, those numbers are appreciably smaller today as well since fewer young people are learning their traditional language.

Whereas Eyak is considered a proto-Athabaskan language (as are 13 other Alaska Native languages including Tlingit), linguists have not been able to relate the Tsimshian language specifically to any other, either of North America or Asia. It does not share certain distinct linguistic characteristics generally associated with all Nadene speakers (excluding Haida). Because of this, Krauss suggests that the language is its own form with no specific relationship or common ancestry to other Alaskan Native languages. A similar linguistic "problem" occurs with Basque which, because of geographical isolation, is unrelated to surrounding languages. Indeed, Hungarian was discovered to have its origins in Finno-Ugric.

Although it is fairly well established just when Tsimshian first came into contact with Europeans, the term "first contact" is a loose term which Peter Nabokov finds is broadly used, but is generally inaccurate. In his *Native American Testimony: A Chronicle of Indian-White Relations from Prophecy to the Present, 1492-1992* (1991), he states that "first contact" was time-relative; that while contact might have been established with one Native group, members of neighboring tribes or nations might well have learned of the white Europeans from Indian traders from "contacted" groups, and thus:

> It is possible that some tribes received advance word of early Indian-white meetings . . . it is important to remember that "first contact," as the initial encounters between Native Americans and whites are termed by anthropologists, occurred at different times in different places. Generally, the more eastern and southern the locale, the earlier was the first contact. Thus the Hopi Indians of Arizona and the Hurons of eastern Canada had both experienced their first meetings with Europeans by about 1540. But the Sioux of the Dakota plains would not have firsthand knowledge of them for another one hundred and fifty years, and the Wintu of northern California for a half century after that. (6)

Whatever Nabokov's argument, it appears that the first Tsimshian-white meeting was established by Russian fur traders around 1830. Although the Russian American Company and the Hudson's Bay Company had been trapping and trading close to the region as of 1826 with the establishment of Fort Connelly on Bear Lake at the head of a branch of the Skeena River, the Tsimshian people had not then been contacted. However, it is entirely likely that metals and tools were traded to the Tsimshian from other native groups which had been contacted earlier (of which Nabokov would agree to have been likely).

It wasn't until 1834 when Fort Simpson was built in British Columbia that whites began their actual influence on the Tsimshian. The Fort attracted other Indian groups as well. The Haida, for instance, came by the hundreds to trade with the English-speaking people. In 1836 the Hudson Bay Company built a post at the north end of Lake Babine and thus the coastal Indians there had a regular trading route.

In 1857 William Duncan was sent by the Church Missionary Society of London to, in the words of Viola Garfield, "christianize and educate the Tsimshian at Fort Simpson." Ten years later, in 1867, he helped found Old Metlakatla some 20 miles from the Fort, but still in British Columbia. He later recognized that the conditions there were so extremely detrimental to the survival of the Tsimshian, that in 1887 he and nearly 1,000 Indians left the colony and established what is now the community of Metlakatla in Alaska. After great difficulties with the Bishop, including Duncan's eventual dismissal from his position, the United States government finally set aside the land for the Tsimshian in 1891. It was and still is the only Indian reservation so designated in Alaska.

Although Duncan learned much of the language and customs of the Natives, the first serious anthopological and linguistic study of the Tsimshian began around 1894 when Franz Boas spent some time conducting field research near Kinkolith for the British Association for the Advancement of Science; and in 1899 he completed a language and ethnography manuscript which was later published in 1902 as *Tsimshian Texts* in which he included English translations of some 23 mythological oral narratives which were originally told and written in Nîsqa'e (Canadian) Tsimshian. From Boas's initial work other studies were conducted, and in the early 1920's William Beynon, a half-breed Tsimshian from Metlakatla, recorded a large volume of oral narratives which were later retranslated and published in an eight-volume collection entitled *Tsimshian Stories* (1980-1985).

I have included in this collection several particularly wonderful oral narratives from Tsimshian. *The Squirrel Shaman* is one of a very small number of tales depicting the magical ritual by which native shamans are created. The *Porcupine and Beaver Story* was first recorded by Boas in1894, and was later translated by W. Beynon in the mid-1920's. The two narratives, *Ko'edhan Volcano Legend* and *The Nass River Volcano* are to me some of the most fascinating tales I have ever collected. Their broad representation throughout Alaskan and north-western Canadian Indian mythologies is suggestive of a catastrophic event(s) some two millenia past which may well have affected New World settlement patterns and Athabaskan languages.

Although the included version of *The Dog-Husband Story* comes from a Canadian Tsimshian storyteller on the Skeena River in British Columbia, similar accounts of the narrative are found in Alaska Tsimshian mythology as well.

(William Duncan's Church in Metlakatla, Circa 1889)

The Squirrel Shaman

This narrative which describes the events that caused a Tsimshian man to become a shaman, was originally told to Franz Boas *in* Nîsqa'e *Tsimshian around 1894 at* Kinkolith *on the* Nass River. *Although Groundhogs appear in some* Eyak *and* Tlingit *myths, this is one of a small number of Alaska Native tales involving squirrels. This narrative is didactic, and like the* Eskimo Ptarmigan Story *it teaches young hunters to have respect for animals.*

In a small village upon the Skeena River, three young brothers would hunt and kill squirrels. They hung the tiny furs to dry and collected the tails. Together they had killed so many squirrels that they had to go further and further away from home to find more.

One day, one of the boys was hunting alone far from the village when he saw a perfectly white squirrel running along the trunk of a very tall tree. The boy raised his bow to shoot, but he saw that it was so pretty that he could not kill this one.

The white squirrel ran into a hole in the tree and turned around and motioned for the boy to follow. The handsome young man appoached and looked inside. He saw that it was a house with a great many empty beds. It was a community house for many people, but there was no one inside. It was entirely empty except for the white squirrel who stood in the middle waving at him to come inside.

"I cannot come in," said the Tsimshian boy. "I am much too big."

"Lean your bow against the Great House, and then you will be able to come inside," replied the white squirrel.

The boy did so and to his surprise he became small enough to walk

into the empty hall. He saw that the white squirrel was a beautiful young woman who was wearing a white fur coat. She told the boy to follow her up to the top of the Great Tree. When they arrived, an old man who looked like a chief spoke to him.

"I have been waiting for you to come. Why have you killed all of my people? All of my children and grandchildren are gone except for my favorite granddaughter who led you to the Great House. Why have you done this?"

The young man looked around and saw that this room too was empty, and then he answered the old chief, "I have not killed your people. I have never killed a person before. I do not know what you are saying old father."

"Look around you," said the chief. "See how we are alone here now where once these halls were full of my people."

The boy looked again and replied, "But I did not kill anyone."

The old man came close to the boy and spoke to him again, "I am the chieftan of the Squirrel People. You and your brothers have killed all of my children and now their skins hang outside your house."

Suddenly the boy understood what had happened. He looked at the girl and saw that she was indeed very beautiful. He felt ashamed and saddened.

"We did not know that you live like people. We did not know that you love your children and grandchildren. I am sorry. Forgive me. I will tell my brothers not to hunt your people any longer."

But the chief was still sad. "It is too late to stop killing us. We are all dead now. My granddaughter and I are all that is left."

"But I did not mean to kill you all!" exclaimed the young hunter as a tear filled his eye. Is there not something I can do?" he asked the old father Squirrel.

"There is a way," said the chief. "I can make you a great shaman and you can return my people."

The young Tsimshian agreed, and so the old man began to work his powerful magic. He took the boy outside and tied his limbs to the tree. Then he pushed sharp needles with string through his skin and pulled them tight in every direction. There was a piercing needle for every dead squirrel. The boy screamed in pain, but the old man said that the pain was part of the power. When he was finished, the chief left the boy hanging for three days. On the third day he returned and sang his magic song for three more days. He did not rest, and he did not eat or drink either. After that, the chief left the boy alone.

One day, the boy's two younger brothers were out hunting squirrels when they came across the carcass of their brother who had been lost for six days. It was hanging in a tall tree just as they had hung the squirrel furs at their house. They cut him down and took his body home.

That night, after they arrived with their dead brother, a magic filled the entire village and all of the dead squirrels came back to life. They ran back to the Great House and told the chief what had happened. After all of the squirrels were returned, the spirit of the young man flew back into his dead body and returned him to life. From that time on, he was a great and powerful shaman and the Tsimshian did not kill squirrels.

Porcupine and Beaver Story

Franz Boas originally documented this myth in 1894 at Kinkolith, *a village on the* Nass River, *while conducting anthropological and linguistic research for the* British Association for the Advancement of Science. *He published this account in* Tsimshian Texts(1902). William Beynon, *a half-breed Tsimshian from* Metlakatla, *later recorded a similar narrative in the mid-1920's. A similar account in* Tlingit *appears in* The Raven And The Totem.

A long time ago animals could speak and a few of them knew magical songs which could change the weather.

Beaver and Porcupine used to be friends until one day when the small porcupine played an awful trick on his friend which almost killed him. Beaver was tricked into climbing to the top of a tree and he fell off and almost died. When he regained his senses, Beaver decided to get revenge.

One day Porcupine went with Beaver to the big lake. When they came to the edge of the lake, Beaver said to his friend, "I will swim under water with you on my back and you will hold your breath all the while."

The little porcupine said, "No, I am scared that I will drown and die in the water."

Beaver replied, "No, you will not drown and die."

Finally, Porcupine agreed to sit on Beaver's back. Beaver dived with the porcupine and they stayed under water so long that Porcupine started to drown. Then Beaver came to the surface and left the near-drowned porcupine on a small island.

Nearly dead, the little porcupine lay there, and when he awoke he saw that he was on a small island on the lake. He was cold and hungry and he wanted to go home. He began to cry.

Then he started to sing a magic song over and over again, "I want to walk to the foot of the mountain."

That night the sky cleared and the air became very cold. Ice formed on the lake's surface. Porcupine kept singing and by morning the ice was thick enough for him to walk upon. He had used his magic to save himself by making the ice come even though it was summer.

The little porcupine walked across the ice to his home.

Although safe, Porcupine was so angry that he thought about singing a song which would bring on a very great cold to kill everyone. But he said to himself, "I care too much for my little children," and so he did not sing the powerful song.

Since that time, beavers and porcupines have not been friends.

Ko'edhan Volcano Legend

Although similar stories exist in Tlingit *and* Haida *mythology, I have included this particular version in this chapter because it was first recorded and translated by* William Beynon, *a* Tsimshian, *in 1948-49 and involves the* Nass River. Dr. William Workman, *an anthropologist at the University of Alaska Anchorage, has for some decades been studying the effects of two volcanic eruptions in southeast Alaska which he believes to have occured at 1,400 and 2,000 years ago. His research, in conjunction with* M. Krauss' *proto-Athabaskan* glottochronology, *suggests that perhaps these two geological catastrophic events caused widespread environmental devastation which eventually forced the Indians of the region to relocate both northward and eastward into Canada. The similarity of narratives from* North-western Canada, *including in* Kutchin', Hare, Dogrib, Yellow-knife, and Chipewyan *mythologies, suggests an Alaskan connection. This particular retelling is based primarily upon the work of both* W. Beynon *and* P. Fast.

There was once a village upon the Nass River. A very long time ago the people there heard strange rumblings coming from the St. Elias mountains. Several warriors were sent to find the source of the rumblings which sounded like drums beating, but they were unable to locate it.

When the noise continued for some time, they sent out another party again and this time they found an abandoned feast house near the base of a mountain. Although the warriors searched, they found nothing and so they returned to their home on the Nass River.

That very night, though, the rumbling continued and this time it was even louder than before. The men returned to the house and they

83

saw men and women dancing and singing inside. They were all naked. None of them were wearing clothes! The men watched for a while and then one of the dancers saw them. The warriors became very frightened and ran home, but they did not tell anyone what they had seen in the feast house at the foot of the mountain.

The rumbling became louder and louder every day. Every night the men returned to the strange house to watch the nude dancers sing, but they did not tell anyone about the place.

After a while, much of the countryside was afire, and streams of lava ran down from the high country where rivers are born. The thunderous rumblings from the mountain were even greater than before. The people of the village along the river were sure to perish if they did not leave soon, but they were too frightened and they did not know where to go.

Finally, the warriors decided to capture one of the strange dancers to find out what was happening. Several of the men entered the house and tried to grab a woman dancer, but their hands went right through her. She was a spirit. They were all ghosts! The ghost-people attacked the men and killed all but one who had protected himself by covering himself with urine, as was their custom before battle or hunting. The survivor ran home and told the villagers what had happened. As soon as he had finished, he fell over dead!

The chief told the people to gather their family and belongings. Then he ordered the evacuation of the entire village. They marched northward and eastward for a very long time, crossing many streams and rivers, and they could see the smoke from the mountain for a great distance.

The Nass River Volcano

In this variation of the Ko'ehdan legend the volcano erupts and destroys the people in punishment for disrespectful acts. Interestingly, these volcano tales are reminiscent in some ways to the Judeo-Christian *story of the* "Tower of Babel." *In that tale mankind is similarly punished, and as a result the common language is lost to numerous languages and dialects.* M. Krauss *has suggested that modern Athabaskan languages, Tlingit and Eyak, had a common origin in what he calls* Proto-Athabaskan-Eyak-Tlingit, *which he believes may have been one language up until some 2,000 years ago, which roughly corresponds to* Workman's *earlier volcanic devastation theory. Perhaps as with* Babel, *the eruption forced not only the dispersal of the peoples, but also caused the ultimate destruction of that common language. According to* Alaska Pacific University *geologist* Dr. Jim Brown, *the 1,800 miles of coastline along the* Gulf of Alaska *is the boundary of the* Pacific Oceanic Plate *to the south and the* North American Plate *to the north. Thus, the coastal region is a subduction zone in which volcanic activity is and has been extremely intense. It is not unexpected that legends relating to volcanoes should exist.*

Once there were several boys who were very cruel to animals and especially to salmon. They lived in a small village on the Nass River where there was always plenty of fish and other foods to eat. The people there were very happy.

It is a long-held belief that the animals and fish must be treated with respect because they give themselves up as food to the Indians who need them to survive. If this taboo is broken, then the violators and their entire village might starve and die as a result of such neglect and cruelty.

85

One summer, when it was spawning time and salmon were crowding the river from bank to bank, these boys would stand on the edge of the water and throw stones at the fish. Sometimes they made sharp spears to throw as well. They did this for the fun of it and if they hurt or killed a fish they did not keep it to eat. They just let it float away.

Soon after that, the villagers began to hear loud sounds like the beating of feast drums. The sounds grew louder and louder until the people were afraid. Finally, from the mountain sprang a river of fire which destroyed everything in its path. The trees were afire and smoke flooded the lowlands.

The people in the village tried to escape, but almost all of them were killed. Those who survived never returned. The village had been destroyed because of the young boys who had broken taboo.

The Dog-Husband Story

This narrative, told by a Canadian Tsimshian *from the* Skeena River, *tells the story of a young woman who unknowingly marries a dog who is mysteriously transformed into human form. Versions of this tale appear in the mythology of the Alaska Tsimshian as well.*

In the long ago, just after the Tsimshian first escaped from Temlax-am in the Interior and travelled down the Skeena River to live where they do nowadays, there was a young woman who was not married. The woman was kind and helped her elder relatives, but she did not have a husband. All that she had was a pet dog which was always with her. At nights, the young woman often spoke to the dog telling him how lonely she was, and how she wished to have a husband so that she could have children.

One morning the dog was missing, and although the woman looked everywhere for him and called his name aloud, she could not find him at all.

That evening a strange man came to the village. No one had ever seen him before. He was really the dog who had turned himself into a man. He asked to marry the young woman and her father agreed.

That night the man and woman slept together for the first time. Soon thereafter the woman became pregnant. It lasted for only a short time before she gave birth to five puppies. The people of the village could not believe their eyes. They knew then that the man was really the lost dog and so they killed him.

Because she had married and slept with a dog, the young woman was abandoned by the village. Several men took her and the five puppies far away and left them stranded on the beach without food or anything.

Raven saw what had happened and he took pity on the poor woman. He made a fire for her so that she was not entirely helpless. Then he helped her build a small house.

Every day the young woman would walk along the shore gathering food for herself and her five children, and every night they would sleep in the small house with the fire that Raven had given to them.

One day, while gathering food, the young woman heard her puppy-children talking inside the house. She crept quietly to the side of the house and looked in through a small hole. There, beside the warm fire, stood the five children in human form. Behind them she could see their dog coats hanging on the wall.

The mother went into the house and threw their dog skins into the fire so that they could not be worn again. By doing that, she forced her children to stay human because they no longer had their dog coats to wear.

With her five human children, the young woman followed the beach for many days until they finally came upon her old village. Because the children were no longer dogs, they were welcomed back. In the years to come they would save the village from starvation and they would eventually all become chiefs.

BIBLIOGRAPHY

The following is a partial list of suggested readings for further information about the oral narratives of the southeast Alaska Native peoples discussed in this book:

Eyak

Alaska Quarterly Review. Vol. 4, No. 3 & 4. Ed. Tom Sexton, Ron Spatz, and James J. Liszka. Anchorage: University of Alaska Anchorage, 1986.

Allen, Henry T. *Report of an Expedition to the Copper, Tanana, and Koyukon Rivers, in the Territory of Alaska, in the year 1885.* Washington: GPO, 1887.

De Laguna, Frederica and Kaj Birket-Smith. *The Eyak Indians Of The Copper River Delta*. Cøpenhagen, 1938.

Johnson, John, Ed. *Eyak Legends of the Copper River Delta, Alaska*. Anchorage: Chugach Heritage Foundation, c. 1991.

Krauss, Michael. *In Honor Of Eyak*. Fairbanks: Alaska Native Language Center, 1982.

-----. "Eyak Text Supplement." Unpublished. 1970-1972.

-----. "Eyak Texts." Mimeo. University of Alaska and Massachusetts Institute of Technology, 1963-1970.

Norman, Howard. *Northern Tales*. New York: Pantheon, 1990.

Smelcer, John E. *Alaska Native Oral Narrative Literature: A Guidebook and Bibliographic Index*. Anchorage: Ahtna Native Corporation and Greenwich UP, 1992.

-----. *Southeast Alaska Native Oral Narrative Literature In Translation*. Ph.D. Dissertation. Hawaii: Greenwich University, 1993.

-----. *A Cycle Of Myths: Native Legends From Southeast Alaska*. Anchorage: Salmon Run, 1993.

Haida

Alaska Quarterly Review. Vol. 4, No. 3 & 4. Ed. Tom Sexton, Ron Spatz, and James J. Liszka. Anchorage: University of Alaska Anchorage, 1986.

Barbeau, Marius. *Haida Myths Illustrated in Argillite Carvings*. Ottawa: National Museum of Canada, No. 127, 1953.

Beck, Mary L. *Heroes & Heroines In Tlingit-Haida Legend*. Seattle: Alaska Northwest, 1989.

Bierhorst, John. *The Mythology of North America*. New York: William Morrow, 1985.

Drew, Leslie. *Haida: Their Art and Culture*. Blaire: Hancock House, 1982.

----- and Douglas Wilson. *The Art Of The Haida*. Vancouver: Hancock House, 1980.

Gridley, Marrion. *The Story Of The Haida*. New York: G. P. Putnam's Sons, 1972.

KIL-KAAS-GIT. Craig: Craig School District, 1973, 1974.

Smelcer, John E. *A Cycle Of Myths: Native Legends From Southeast Alaska.* Anchorage: Salmon Run, 1993.

-----. *Alaska Native Oral Narrative Literature: A Guidebook and Bibliographic Index.* Anchorage: Ahtna Native Corporation, 1992.

Swanton, John R. *Contributions to the Ethnology of the Haida.* Washington: American Museum of Natural History 8, 1905.

-----. *Haida Texts and Myths.* Washington: Bureau of American Ethnology, Bul. 29, 1905.

----- and Franz Boas. *Haida Songs. Tsimshian Texts.* Washington: American Ethnological Society, Vol. 3, 1912.

The Man Who Became an Eagle. Retold by J. Enrico. British Columbia UP, 1984

Wherry, Joseph H. *Indian Masks And Myths Of The West.* New York: Funk & Wagnell, 1969.

Xadaas (Haida). Becky Bear, Ed. Hydaburg: Hydaburg Schools, 1982.

Tlingit

Ackerman, Maria. *Tlingit Stories.* Anchorage: Alaska Pacific UP, 1975.

Alaska Quarterly Review. Vol. 4, No. 3 & 4. Ed. Tom Sexton, Ron Spatz, James J. Liszka. Anchorage: University of Alaska Anchorage, 1986.

Allen, Henry T. *Report of an Expedition to the Copper, Tanana, and Koyukon Rivers, in the Territory of Alaska, in the Year 1885.* Washington: GPO, 1887.

Beck, Mary L. *Heroes & Heroines In Tlingit-Haida Legend.* Seattle: Alaska Northwest Books, 1989.

-----. *Shamans and Kushtakas.* Seattle: Alaska Northwest, 1991.

Bernet, John W., Ed. *An Anthology Of Aleut, Eskimo, And Indian Literature Of Alaska.* Fairbanks: University of Alaska Fairbanks, English Department, 1974.

Carter, M. *Legends, Tales & Totems.* Palmer: Aladdin Press, 1975.

Dauenhauer, Nora and Richard. *Haa Shuka; Our Ancestors.* Juneau: University of Washington Press, 1987.

-----. *Haa Tuwunaaqu Yis: For Healing Our Spirit.* Seattle: Washington UP, 1990.

Dolch, Edward W. and Marguerite. *Stories From Alaska: Folklore of the World.* Illinois: Garrard Press, 1961.

Dundes, Alan. *Folklore Theses and Dissertations in the United States.* Austin: Texas UP, 1976.

Emmons, George T. *Memoirs of the American Museum of Natural History.* Vol. III, 1900-1907.

De Laguna, Frederica. *Under Mount Saint Elias: The History and Culture of the Yakutat Tlingit.* Washington: Smithsonian, 1972.

Fast, Phyllis A. *Naatsilanei And Ko'ehdan: A Semiotic Analysis Of Two Alaska Native Myths*. MFA thesis. Anchorage: University of Alaska Anchorage, 1990.

Feldmann, Susan. Ed.' *The Story-Telling Stone*. New York: Dell, 1991.

Garfield, Viola E. and Linn A. Forest. *The Wolf and the Raven*. Seattle: Washington UP, 1949.

Hallock, Charles. *Our New Alaska*. New York: Forest and Stream Publishing Company, 1886.

Harris, Christie. *Once More Upon A Totem*. New York: Atheneum, 1973.

Harris, Lorle K. *Tlingit Tales*. California: Naturegraph, 1985.

Holmberg, H. J. *Holmberg's Ethnographic Sketches*. Trans. F. Jaensch. Fairbanks: University of Alaska Press, 1985.

Jonaitis, Aldona. *Art of the Northern Tlingit*. Seattle: Washington UP, 1986.

Jones, Livingston F. *A Study of the Thlingets of Alaska*. New York: Fleming H. Revell, 1914.

Kamenskii, Anatolii. *Tlingit Indians Of Alaska*. Trans. Sergei Kan. Fairbanks: University of Alaska Press, 1985.

Kapier, Dan and Nan Kapier. *Tlingit: Their Art, Culture & Legends*. Seattle: Hancock House, 1978.

Keithahn, Edward L. *Monuments in Cedar*. Ketchikan, 1945.

Krause, Aurel. *The Tlingit Indians*. Trans. Erna Gunther. Seattle:
Washington UP, 1970.

Krenov, Julia. "Legends from Alaska." *Journal de la Societe des
Americanistes*, n.s. 40 (1951): 173-95.

Leer, J., Ed. *Tongass Texts*. Fairbanks: University of Alaska-
Fairbanks Alaska Native Language Center, 1978.

Lynch, Kathleen. *Southeastern Stories*. Anchorage: Adult Literacy
Laboratory, 1978.

Martin, Fran. *Nine Tales Of Raven*. New York: Harper & Row,
1951.

Mayol, Lurline B. *The Talking Totem Pole*. Portland: Binfords &
Mort, 1943.

McClellan, Catherine. *The Girl Who Married The Bear: A
Masterpiece of Indian Oral Tradition*. Ottawa: Canadian
National Museum Publication, 1970.

-----. "Inland Tlingit." *Subarctic*, Vol. 6, 1981.

McCorckle, Ruth. *The Alaska Ten Footed Bear And Other
Legends*. Seattle: Robert D. Seal, 1958.

Norman, Howard. *Northern Tales: Traditional Tales of Eskimo
and Indian Peoples*. New York: Pantheon Books, 1990.

Paul, Frances L. *Kahtahah*. Anchorage: Alaska Northwest, 1976.

Peck, Cyrus and Nadja Peck. *The Rocks Of Our Land Speak*.
Juneau: Juneau Douglas School District, 1977.

Peck, Cyrus E., Sr. *The Tides People*. Juneau: Indian Studies Program. Juneau School District, 1975.

Postell, Alice and A.P. Johnson. *Tlingit Legends*. Sitka: Sheldon Jackson Museum, 1986.

Smelcer, John. Ed. *The Raven and the Totem: Traditional Alaska Native Myths and Tales*. Anchorage: Salmon Run, 1992.

-----. *Alaska Native Oral Narrative Literature: A Guidebook and Bibliographic Index*. Anchorage: Ahtna Native Corporation and Greenwich UP, 1992.

-----. *A Cycle Of Myths: Native Legends From Southeast Alaska*. Anchorage: Salmon Run, 1993.

Swanton, John R. *Tlingit Myths and Texts*. Washington: U. S. Bureau of American Ethnology, 1909.

Trask, Willard R. *The Unwritten Song*, Vol. II. New York: Macmillian, 1967.

Velten, H. "Three Tlingit Stories." *International Journal of American Linguistics*. 10 (1944): 168-180.

Zuboff, Robert. *Kudatan Kahidee (The Salmon Box)*. Trans. Henry Davis. Sitka: Tlingit Readers, 1973.

-----. *Taax'aa (Mosquito)*. Ed. and Trans. Dick Dauenhauer. Fairbanks: University of Alaska Fairbanks, Alaska Native Language Center, 1973.

Tsimshian

Angus, Charlotte, et al. *We-gyet Wanders On: Legends of the Northwest*. Seattle: Hancock House, 1977.

Beynon, William. *Tsimshian Stories. Vol. I-VIII.* Metlakatla: Metlakatla Indian Community, 1980-1985.

Bierhorst, John. *The Mythology of North America*. New York: William Morrow, 1985.

Boas, Franz. *Tsimshian Texts*. Washington: GPO, Bureau of American Ethnology, Bul. 27, 1902.

-----. *Tsimshian Mythology*. Washington: Bureau of American Ethnology, Report 31, 1916.

-----. *Tsimshian. Handbook of American Indian Languages.* Bureau of American Ethnology, 1930.

Cove, John. *Shattered Images: Dialogues And Meditations On Tsimshian Narratives*. Ottawa: Carleton UP, 1987.

Garfield, Viola E. and Paul S. Wingert. *The Tsimshian Indians And Their Arts.* Seattle: Washington UP, 1950. Reprint, 1966.

Niblack, Albert P. *The Coast Indians of Southern Alaska and Northern British Columbia.* Report of the U. S. National Museum, 1890.

Shotridge, L. "A Visit to the Tsimshian Indians." *Museum Journal,* Vol. 10. Pennsylvania UP, 1919.

Smelcer, John E. *Alaska Native Oral Narrative Literature: A Guidebook and Bibliographic Index.* Anchorage: Ahtna Native Corporation and Greenwich UP, 1992.

-----. *Southeast Alaska Native Oral Narrative Literature in T ranslation.* Ph.D. Dissertation. Hawaii: Greenwich University, 1993.

-----. *A Cycle Of Myths: Native Legends From Southeast Alaska.* Anchorage: Salmon Run, 1993.

SOPE: A Tsimshian Story. Anchorage: National Bilingual Materials Development Center, 1978.

Swanton, John R. *Haida Songs. Tsimshian Texts.* Washington: American Ethnological Society, 1912.

Wherry, Joseph H. *Indian Masks And Myths Of The West.* New York: Funk & Wagnell, 1969.

Index

BOOK ORDER FORM

These fine books are available at most bookstores, or use this handy order form:

A Cycle Of Myths:
Native Legends From Southeast Alaska
ISBN 0-9634000-2-9
By John E. Smelcer $12.95

Alaska Native Oral Narrative Literature:
A Guidebook and Bibliographic Index
ISBN 0-9634000-4-5
By John E. Smelcer $12.95

The Raven And The Totem:
Traditional Alaska Native Myths And Tales
ISBN 0-9634000-0-2
By John E. Smelcer $14.95

Please send me the above title(s). I am enclosing $____ and $1.00 per book for postage and shipping. Send check or money order to:

SALMON RUN PUBLISHERS™
P.O. Box 231081
Anchorage, AK 99523-1081

Please allow two to three weeks for delivery.

About The Artists

John E. Smelcer, PhD has taught at numerous colleges and universities throughout the world and was recently the Guest Native American Scholar at the Gorky Institute of World Literature in Moscow, Russia where he also lectured at Moscow State University and Lenin College.

His books on Alaska Native myths include *The Raven and the Totem, A Cycle of Myths,* and *Alaska Native Oral Narrative Literature in Translation.* He is the author of numerous encyclopedic essays on Alaska Native and Native American cultures and history.

His family on his father's side is Ahtna Athabaskan Indian, one of the twenty culturally-unique tribes in Alaska. His mother has some Cherokee ancestry. Dr. Smelcer has written a collection of poetry written in the Ahtna language. The book, *Koht'aene Kenaege',* is the only such collection in print.

His poems have appeared in *The Atlantic Monthly, The American Voice, The Amicus Journal, The Christian Science Monitor, The Beloit Poetry Journal, The International Poetry Review, Poet,* and *The Kenyon Review.*

Larry Vienneau teaches Art at the University of Alaska Fairbanks and has also taught at Bridgewater State College in Massachussetts. His artwork has received national acclaim and have been showcased in numerous national and international exhibits to include a recent show in Hong Kong. He received the *Best of Painting Award* at the 1992 All Alaska Juried Art Show. His wife, Suhtling, recently earned her graduate degree in film-making and has worked abroad in Hong Kong and in China.